D is for Dancing Dragon
A China Alphabet

Written by Carol Crane and Illustrated by Zong-Zhou Wang

*My many thanks to Irene Yi Ross; Beth Johnston, my sister, and her husband,
Roger, who were residents of Shanghai; and Polly Clausen, my niece,
a teacher in Shanghai for ten years. They were great resources for this book.*

CAROL

*A gift for American kids who
love Chinese culture.*

ZONG-ZHOU

Text Copyright © 2006 Carol Crane
Illustration Copyright © 2006 Zong-Zhou Wang

Sleeping Bear Press™

310 North Main Street, Suite 300
Chelsea, MI 48118
www.sleepingbearpress.com

THOMSON
★
GALE™

© 2006 Thomson Gale, a part of the Thomson Corporation.

Thomson, Star Logo and Sleeping Bear Press are trademarks
and Gale is a registered trademark used herein under license.

Printed and bound in China.

10 9 8 7 6 5 4 3 2 1

Library of Congress Cataloging-in-Publication Data

Crane, Carol.
D is for dancing dragon : a China alphabet / written by Carol Crane;
illustrated by Zong Wang.
p. cm.
Summary: "This A to Z children's pictorial covers topics such as Beijing, Dragon Dance, Himalayan
Mountain Range, Mongolians, and the giant panda. Each subject is introduced with a simple rhyme
for younger readers. Expository text is also included for older readers"—Provided by publisher.
ISBN 1-58536-273-5
1. China—Civilization—Juvenile literature. I. Title.

DS721.C865 2006
951—dc22   2006001426

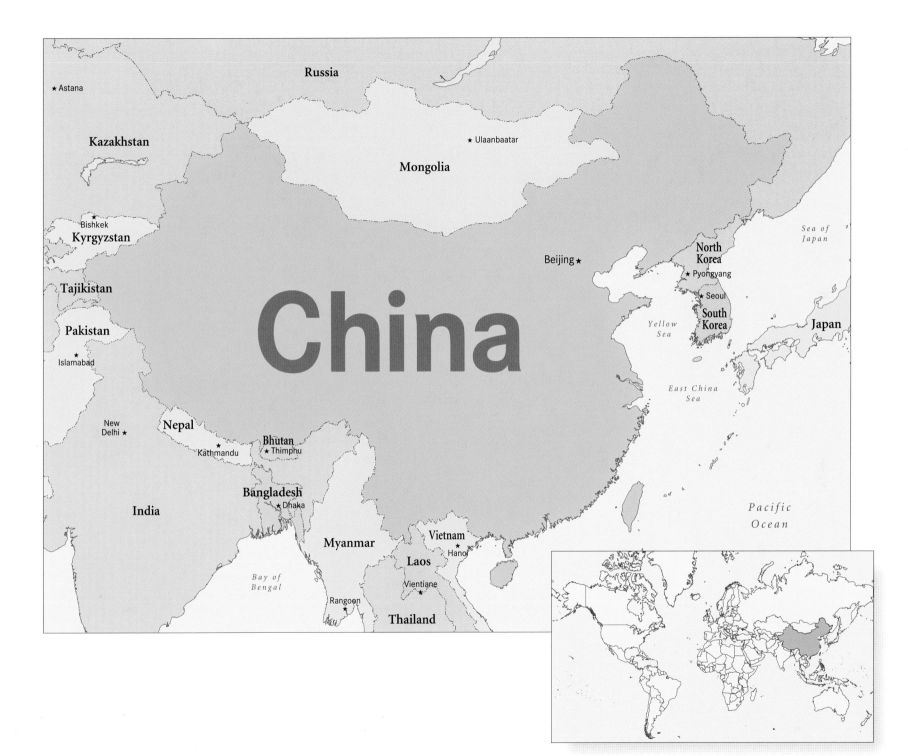

Chinese acrobats have been performing for more than 2,000 years. They have perfected daring feats as audiences clap and cheer. Rope walking, juggling with both hands and feet, and the human pagoda (which is standing on each others' shoulders in a triangle) are a few of their amazing acts. Running quickly and then soaring through the air, the acrobats seem light as small birds. Caught by one of the other performers, or landing gracefully, they are ready to take flight again.

The acrobats' physical strength and stamina are astounding. In early days they performed in festivals. Later Beijing formed a troupe of the most outstanding acrobats from each major city in China. Today their astonishing skills are known worldwide.

A is for Chinese Acrobats
performing with beauty and grace.
We clap and admire their physical strength,
as they land in a very small place.

A a

Beijing is the capital of the People's Republic of China. It is one of the largest cities in China with a population of around twelve million people. Beijing enjoys a sub-tropical winter, but it can be very hot and dry in the summer because of the winds from the Gobi Desert. Visitors that come to learn about the culture and history of Beijing may find there is too much to see in one trip. Beijing has museums, palaces, gardens, and ancient relics of man's existence thousands of years ago.

Tiananmen Square is the largest public square in the world. Families and visitors take walks on the 99-acre (4-hectare) square. The square was built to accommodate one million people. In the middle of the square is the Monument to the People's Heroes. Across the street is Tiananmen Gate, which leads to the Forbidden City. The Imperial Palace, also known as the "Forbidden City" (so named as the common people were forbidden to enter) or Gu Gong, was the imperial residence during the reign of 24 emperors.

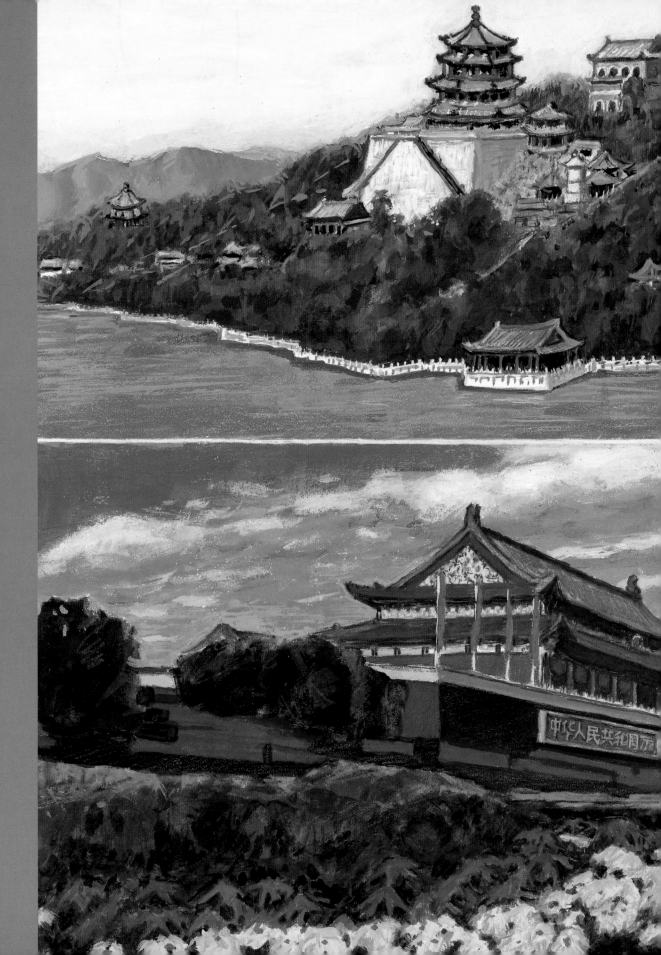

Yellow is the symbol of the royal family and it is the predominant color at the Imperial Palace. Emperors wore yellow gowns that had dragons embroidered on them. Surrounding the palace is a high wall, a moat (a wide trench filled with water), and over 800 buildings that contain 8,886 rooms. Also in this area is the Great Hall of the People and the National History Museum. The Summer Palace, once a residence of emperors in summer, has an imperial garden with a lake, bridges, and islands with beautiful flowers. Beautiful Beijing—home of the Olympic Games in 2008.

B is for Beijing.
Big in size, culture, and history,
it is the capital of China.
Why visitors love it is no mystery.

Bb

C is for Chopsticks
an ancient eating skill.
Bamboo sticks called "quick little fellows."
How do you eat and not spill?

Cc

Chopsticks have been used in China for over 5,000 years. Many years ago cooking was done mostly over wood or coal burning fires. Sticks were used to pull the food out of the fire. Later when coal and firewood became scarce, the food was cut into smaller pieces so it would cook faster. The twigs that had been used to pull food from the fire became wooden tapered chopsticks for eating. Many chopsticks are made from bamboo or wood. Ivory chopsticks were used for banquets. The royal family often used gold chopsticks. The Chinese chopsticks are 9 to 10 inches (23 to 25.5 centimeters) long, rectangular in shape, and have blunt ends. Picking up small things such as rice, beans, and slippery noodles takes practice. It is thought that using chopsticks has a great deal in common with writing Chinese characters with a brush. Both eating and writing have become an artful skill in China.

When a guest is invited to a Chinese home, etiquette is considered to be very important. Chopsticks should always be placed on the dish, never in the bowl of rice. It is considered rude to tap a bowl with chopsticks. The host or hostess also shows respect to their guest by following proper etiquette. The spout of a teapot will never be pointed toward any guest as this is considered bad luck. The number four is considered bad luck so there will never be four chairs at a table. There are also no fourth-floor buttons on elevators.

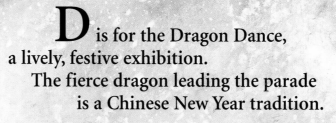

D is for the Dragon Dance,
a lively, festive exhibition.
The fierce dragon leading the parade
is a Chinese New Year tradition.

The Chinese New Year's Dragon Dance celebrates the dragon, believed to bring good fortune, longevity, strength, and wisdom. All communities in China have dragons in their annual festivals. The dragon looks very fierce and is considered the divine ruler of the lakes, rivers, and seas. It is believed to be a powerful but gentle creature that brings rain to the earth, helps the crops grow, and keeps the farmer cool. The size and length of the dragon depends on how many dancers are available to put on the dragon costume. Some dragons are 7 sections long and some can be 46 sections long and need up to 65 dancers to hold up the poles attached to the material of the dragon. Some of the decorations on the dragon are very heavy. When the beat of drums and gongs is heard, the dragon pursues the "Precious Pearl," a symbol of wisdom. The pearl is at the head of the dragon. The dancers underneath have to watch for signals. They know the correct footsteps cannot be too fast or too slow. Every movement must be made in a synchronized plan.

In ancient days the dragon was regarded as a most sacred animal and could only be used on the gowns of emperors. Today dragon symbols are seen in restaurants, on dishes, embroidered on clothing, and painted on walls.

E is for Ehru

a Chinese wooden two-stringed fiddle.
It is one of many musical instruments
known to children when they are little.

Ee

Music is very important in China. Children take piano and violin lessons hoping to be able to play in the youth orchestra someday. Children are taught about the old instruments that were played by their families long ago. The *ehru* [AY-roo] is similar to the fiddle, but instead of having four strings it has two. The *Pipa* is an orchestra instrument that when played can make the sound of horses galloping, or the sounds of a battlefield. It has four or five strings that are played *Pi* (forward) and *Pa* (backward). A lute is similar to a guitar. The moon lute is round like the moon and even has two eyes and a mouth like the moon. One of the oldest instruments is the *sheng*. It consists of bamboo pipes of different lengths that are mounted together on a base. Music is produced by blowing and sucking air through a tube in the base. Children also learn to play the bronze bells that were invented by China over 3,000 years ago.

F is for the "Four Treasures of Study"— the brush, ink stick, paper, and ink stone.
A student needs these tools for writing, for the art of calligraphy is well known.

Calligraphy is a major subject for students from elementary to high school. It is a form of writing that has been used in China for a long time. The Chinese written language has over 50,000 characters. Every word is represented by one character, and the characters are written from top to bottom. The main tool that is used in calligraphy is a brush because brushes can move freely from side to side and up and down. Brushes are made from fine, soft animal hair. The ink stick is made from a mixture of soot and resin. The perfect paper for calligraphy absorbs the ink but does not spread it from the brush. Ink stones are very smooth. A calligrapher will put water on the stone and then rub the ink stick over the stone until the ink is ready for the brush.

Children begin learning calligraphy when they are around six years old. Calligraphy has become an art form. Many famous poets, lyricists, and writers use calligraphy to tell a story or write a poem. When finished they sign their works with a red seal. This signifies the paper is authentic by that artist.

F f

Gg

G is for the Great Wall,
  built over two thousand years ago.
Winding up and down mountains
  and keeping out the Emperor's foe.

The Great Wall of China is the longest structure ever built. It is about 4,000 miles (6,437 kilometers) long. It was built entirely by hand over 2,000 years ago. The construction of the wall continued for centuries and required the work of millions of Chinese.

The word *Qin* is pronounced "ch'in," which is the source of the name China. The wall was a symbol of Emperor Qin's strength and provided defense from the Mongols of the north and other invading enemies. The Emperor wanted the wall to be six horses wide at the top, eight horses wide at the bottom, and five men high. The wall was built with stone, mud, and bricks. It winds like a long dragon across deserts, mountains, and grasslands.

The Great Wall can be seen from space, but contrary to popular legend, it cannot be seen from the moon. Today visitors walk the wall and can experience the history of this man-made wonder.

H h

All of the world's highest mountain peaks are located in the Himalayan Mountain Range. This vast mountain range is located on the continent of Asia and forms the southwest border of China. Astronauts can see the mountain range from their space shuttles.

The highest peak is Mount Everest, which is as high as jets fly when reaching their cruising altitudes, about 5 miles (8 kilometers) high. Mount Everest is in Nepal on the border of Tibet. It was formed about sixty million years ago. Mount Everest was named after Sir George Everest, the British surveyor-general of India, in 1865. He was the first person to record the height and location of Mount Everest. In Nepal the peak is called *Sagarmatha*, meaning "goddess of the sky," and in Tibet it is named *Chomolungma* meaning "mother goddess of the land."

H is for the Himalayan Mountain Range.
Climbers have made it their quest
to scale a mountain of great size—
most famous is Mount Everest.

Due to geological forces, Mount Everest rises a few millimeters each year. In the summer the Himalayan Mountain Range is a barrier to heavy masses of humid air caused by monsoons. In winter the mountain range blocks cold winds from entering too far into central China. The Himalayas have also been a natural barrier to the movement of people in bordering countries. Therefore neighboring countries do not share China's language and customs.

China has given the world many inventions. Some of these were made thousand of years ago. Many of the items in our everyday lives were invented in China, including the paper used to print this book. Ts'ai Lun, an official of the Imperial court, is credited as the inventor of paper. He combined bamboo fibers and the inner bark of a mulberry tree and found that when mixed with water, they made a substance called pulp. He then poured the mixture onto a flat piece of coarsely woven cloth and let the water drain through. When the remaining pulp was solid enough, he lifted it off the cloth and hung it up to dry. He found that he had created a writing surface. The Chinese also found a special way to apply ink to paper. This invention was called printing.

I is for Chinese Inventions.
Paper, the first compass, and more—
abacus, wheelbarrows, and fireworks, too,
discoveries never known before.

device for launching gunpowder

process for papermaking and printing

compass

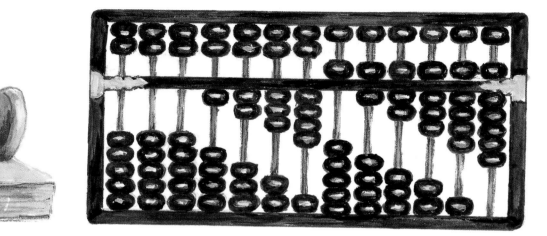

abacus

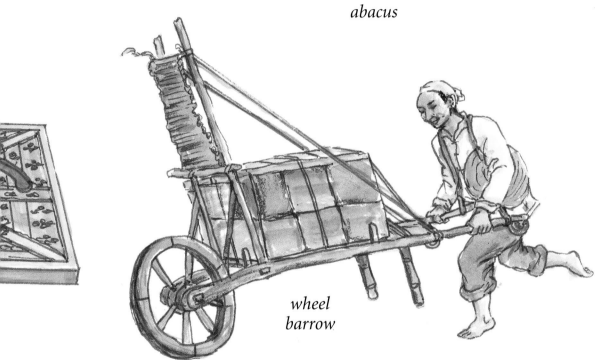

wheel barrow

The compass is a tool with a magnetized needle that aligns itself with the magnetic fields of the Earth. The compass was used in early maritime travel for navigation. The Chinese also came up with a tool to help with math. This invention was called the abacus. It is the oldest kind of calculating machine in the world. The abacus has been tested and is able to get an answer faster than a calculator!

Gardeners use wheelbarrows to move dirt, stones, and plants. This one-wheeled cart was invented in China almost 2,000 years ago. Fireworks were also invented in China 1,000 years ago. Early inventors found if they filled small bamboo rods with different chemicals they began to spark and explode when lit. These are just a few of the many inventions the Chinese people have contributed to the world.

Flower merchants by the hundreds and thousands stream through the city gates every morning to set up their flower stalls. The market is filled with brilliant colors, sweet scents, and cut flowers. Since the earliest times, flowers have been cultivated so that blooms can be enjoyed year round. One emperor had jasmine planted around his palace grounds so he could enjoy its fragrance. Jasmine blooms in both white and yellow. There are bouquets of roses, mostly red, as it is considered a lucky color in China. In the spring peonies and day-lilies are available. Lotus ponds scent the air for miles around and the lotus flower can also be purchased on the street. Many poems have been written about the lotus flower. It grows out of the mud under the water and blooms into a beautiful flower that represents beauty and freshness. The chrysanthemum and Chinese rose are Beijing's official city flowers. The scholar tree and the oriental cypress are the official city trees. The imperial families enjoyed flowers every day. The gardeners used heated brick beds for warming the ground and tricked flowers into blooming even in cold months.

J j

J is for Jasmine,
the aroma is so sweet,
one of the beautiful flowers
we see on Market Street.

Jasmine tea is a favorite flavor in summer as it is said to relieve the inner heat in your body. Jasmine tea is made by layering tea leaves with fresh jasmine petals to absorb their scent. According to legend tea was discovered 5,000 years ago by China's emperor, Sheng Nung. During his time water was often boiled before drinking for hygienic reasons. One day a few leaves from a nearby bush blew into his cup of hot water. He drank some of this new beverage and decided that he liked its aroma and flavor. This is the story of how tea was created. Jasmine tea is the oldest of the scented teas and is still one of the most popular teas today.

Kites were invented in China thousands of years ago. One legend suggests that during a strong wind, a hat flew off the head of a man who was trying to keep birds out of his rice field. He thought it would be great if he could use something like a hat to scare away the birds. So he tied a string to the hat. Then he held onto the string and the kite was born! There are many sizes and varieties of kites with various painted designs like dragons, flowers, birds, and butterflies. Bamboo was placed on the frame of the kite to give it more strength. The Chinese call kites *fengzheng*. Years ago a bamboo whistle was attached to the frame of the kite. It made a sound like the *zheng*, a musical instrument much like the zither. *Feng* means wind so kites in China are called fengzheng.

In addition to kite making, the Chinese people are known for their many amazing art pieces. Paper cutting is an old art form. Turning the paper this way and that, cutting a large piece of paper into a picture, the artist can make birds, pandas, crickets, and flowers come alive in just a few minutes. Cutouts can be made into window decorations, festival scenes, or three-dimensional landscapes. Up to a dozen pieces of paper are used when the artist starts cutting out a scene.

Soaring higher and higher,
just about out of sight.
Bright-colored designs with flowing tails,
the letter K is for Kite.

The Chinese people used knot tying to record events. This form of art has become a way to tie and place jewels in knots for wearing either around the neck or placing on walls as decorations. Threads or cords knotted in a geometric pattern is called *macramé*. Since ancient times, macramé has decorated emperor and empress chairs, edges of parasols, as well as eyeglass cases, fans, and mirrors.

Dough has been a favorite of children all over the world for making all sorts of imaginative things. The Chinese people have been making dough figurines for over 2,000 years. The artists mold tiny figures so small they can be placed in a walnut shell half. This folk art shows men and women in full Chinese kimonos and scenes from emperors' palaces. Small dogs, the Pekingese and the Shar-pei, are made from dough and seen at the emperor's side. These breeds came from China over 2,000 years ago.

K
k

L is for Lanterns—
luminaries children have made—
gathering at nighttime,
in a twinkling parade.

Ll

The Lantern Festival is celebrated on the fifteenth day of the Spring Festival, marking the end of the Chinese New Year celebrations. Children display their lanterns in a nighttime parade. Often children compete in contests to see who can design the most beautiful lanterns. Designs with panda bears, lions, dragons, and flowers are painted on the lanterns. Others will choose the animals of the zodiac. Many children choose red paper for their lanterns. Many Chinese people in other countries also celebrate this day.

M is for Mongolians,
wandering nomads to the north,
herding goats, sheep, cattle, and horses
on grasslands back and forth.

The nomads that live in the north of China are descendants of the famous Mongols. During the thirteenth century, Mongolian leader Genghis Khan, his sons, and then his grandson, Kublai Khan, conquered all of Asia and Eastern Europe. The Mongolians live in yurts, which are round tents with a lattice framework covered with animal hide. The inside of the yurts are decorated with beautifully woven tapestries and carpets. The nomads move from place to place as they lead their livestock to new grasslands. Even though some of the Mongolians have settled in Chinese cities, most still honor the importance of their traditional ways. Once a year they gather on the grasslands and show the skills of their ancestors. They compete in games with excellent horse-manship, archery, and wrestling just as in the time of Genghis Khan.

M
m

The Chinese New Year, also known as the Spring Festival, is a 15-day celebration that signals the end of winter and the coming of spring. Because the Chinese calendar is based on the cycles of the sun and moon, the start of the new year falls on a different day each year. It usually takes place somewhere between the end of January and February, beginning with the second new moon after the winter solstice and ending with the full moon 15 days later.

Families prepare their home for the festival. It is cleaned and swept and then the broom is put away so good luck will not be swept out. The window frames and doors are painted with a new coat of red paint. The house is decorated with paper cutouts and banners are hung on the doors. Folk art prints may have cranes or peaches symbolizing a long life, or the plum or peony that brings good fortune and happiness. The New Year's Eve supper is a feast with all members of the family gathering together. Chicken and fish are prepared. Noodles are served uncut to represent long life. One favorite dessert is a dumpling made of flour, rolled into balls, and stuffed with a sweet filling of peanuts or sesame.

N n

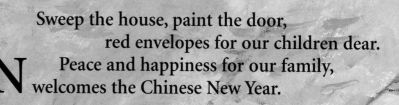

Sweep the house, paint the door,
  red envelopes for our children dear.
Peace and happiness for our family,
N welcomes the Chinese New Year.

The trains are crowded with families traveling to be together for this occasion. The shops in most cities are closed to honor the New Year's celebration. Firecrackers are set off everywhere, and lion and dragon dances are performed in the cities and villages. Very early in the morning on the first day of the new year, the children are given lucky red envelopes with money inside.

There are many ancient beliefs practiced on New Year's Day in China. It is thought to be bad luck to wash your hair because you would wash out the good luck for the new year. If you cry on New Year's Day, you will cry all year long, and you must be extra nice to dogs on the second day since it is thought to be every dog's birthday. Sometimes families exchange gifts. When guests are invited to someone's home, they bring oranges and tangerines to give to the host or hostess—these fruits symbolize abundant happiness. An important part of the New Year's celebration is to honor and respect past ancestors.

Painted faces and colorful costumes
are all part of the musical show.
Marionettes and glove puppets, too—
Chinese Opera is our O.

Oo

Legends and historical events in Chinese history are acted out in either comic or sad performances. A story is told by singers and dancers dressed in beautiful costumes. The painted faces show if the characters are heroes or villains. A red face shows bravery and loyalty, a purple face shows nobility, a black face shows a bold character, and a green face shows a total lack of self restraint. Clowns' faces are painted white with a black patch, whereas an all-white face shows the villain. Actors may also wear wooden masks to tell a story. Long white sleeves of satin look like ripples in water and are a great part of the actors' costumes. Swinging the sleeves back and forth represents signs of anger, rippling and shivering the sleeves shows fear, and letting the sleeves fall forward implies there is going to be a disaster.

Children and adults love the puppet show. There are three types of puppetry. The string marionettes are the oldest. These costumed puppets dance across the stage controlled by strings. Shadow puppetry is performed behind a thin sheet of cloth illuminated from behind by a bright light. This creates silhouettes of the puppets. Glove, or bag, puppets are made to perform somersaults, martial arts, and acrobatics.

P p

P is for the giant panda,
living in the forests of bamboo.
In the wild, pandas are found only in China.
Worldwide they may be found in a zoo.

Giant pandas are one of the most endangered species on Earth with only around 1,000 still living in the wild. There are a few zoos around the world that have pandas in captivity. The Chinese government loans pandas to zoos in other countries so all countries can study the panda and try to protect it.

The panda is a mammal covered with thick, woolly fur. It is mostly white with black fur around its eyes and covering its shoulders, legs, and ears. The panda resembles both a bear and a raccoon. For years scientists believed the panda was related to the raccoon family, but newer research shows that it is more closely related to bears. Some scientists think the panda is in a family all its own. The Chinese name for the giant panda means "great bear cat."

Pandas live in the mountains of China where it can get very cold during the winter months. Their paws are covered with fur to keep them warm and to help the panda grip the ice- and snow-covered ground. A full-grown panda weighs between 165 and 350 pounds (75 and 160 kilograms). Baby pandas are very fragile and weigh only 3 to 5 ounces (85 to 142 grams) at birth. They are all white when they are born and develop their black spots after about a month. Baby pandas are weaned at around 9 months but often stay with their mothers for up to 18 months.

The giant panda has very strong jaws and teeth to crush bamboo, its main food source. Climbing up into and hiding in the forests of bamboo, it eats 20 to 40 pounds (9 to 18 kilograms) of bamboo per day. It munches and crunches and continuously eats for 10 to 16 hours a day. The biggest threat to the panda is the widespread destruction of its natural habitat. The bamboo forests have become smaller and smaller due to a grow-ing human population.

Q is for the Qin Terra-Cotta Warriors and Horses,
a buried treasure found from long ago.
Each soldier is dressed and ready for battle,
standing in formations all in a row.

Around seven hundred thousand workers spent more than 30 years building the underground tomb of the emperor, Qin. In 1974 farmers were digging a well and uncovered pieces of pottery. After the farmers notified the authorities of their find, archeologists (scientists who study artifacts from long ago) came to the area and uncovered life-size horses, chariots, and warriors made of terra-cotta pottery. So far more than 7,000 terra-cotta warriors have been found and restored. The figures are all life-size and each face has its own expression. There are officers and soldiers holding spears and swords and soldiers steering full-size, horse-drawn chariots into battle. All of these figures are the replicas of what the imperial guard looked like in the young emperor's time. He had wanted his army to always be with him, even after his death.

The museum of Qin Terra-Cotta Warriors and Horses is open to the public in Xi'an where this historical display can be honored and viewed.

Qq

R r

China is a very large country. It is the third largest in the world in land area after Russia and Canada, and the largest in population. The farmers of China are very important. They grow the food that feeds the most populated country in the world, more than one billion people. Rice is one of this country's major crops. It takes a lot of hard work to grow rice. Water buffaloes are used to plow the fields in wet areas. They sink up to their knees in mud as they slowly pull the plow. The water buffalo is not used in dry areas as they need lots of water to drink. Rice seeds are planted in a muddy field. When the rice shoots, or plants, are tall enough they are then transplanted into a larger field. This field, or paddy, is irrigated, which is a way to bring clean water to dry land. The paddies are carefully controlled to ensure the proper depth of water. Chinese farmers invented the chain pump to aid with irrigation. The farmers would pump water into the fields by walking on paddles much like a bicycle. It worked! Last, the farmers drain the fields, cut and dry the rice stalks, separate the kernels of rice from the stalks, and store it.

R is for Rice paddies
where farmers work to grow grain.
Here are vast squares of water and green
on hillsides or level terrain.

The Silk Road was important for exchanging goods and learning about different cultures. From Asia came silk, paper, bamboo, jade, and gunpowder and from Europe came colored glass, woolen rugs, horses, and strange unknown birds and animals. The Silk Road was not really a single road. It was a series of routes linking China and the Roman Empire. Thousands of miles (kilometers) of cold, steep mountain passes and hot empty deserts with sandstorms made up the Silk Road. Sometimes bandits were along the hazardous lengthy route. The two-humped Bactrian camel could carry 400 to 500 pounds (181 to 227 kilograms) of merchandise. There could be 1,000 camels in the caravan traveling along at a snail's pace. China had discovered silk and the Roman Empire wanted it. The Silk Road was an active trade route until about the fifteenth century when a water route was discovered that linked Asia with Europe, which ended the need for the Silk Road.

S s

S is for the Silk Road.
        Caravans traveling mile after mile
trading silk, jade, and bamboo,
            burdened camels moving in a slow style.

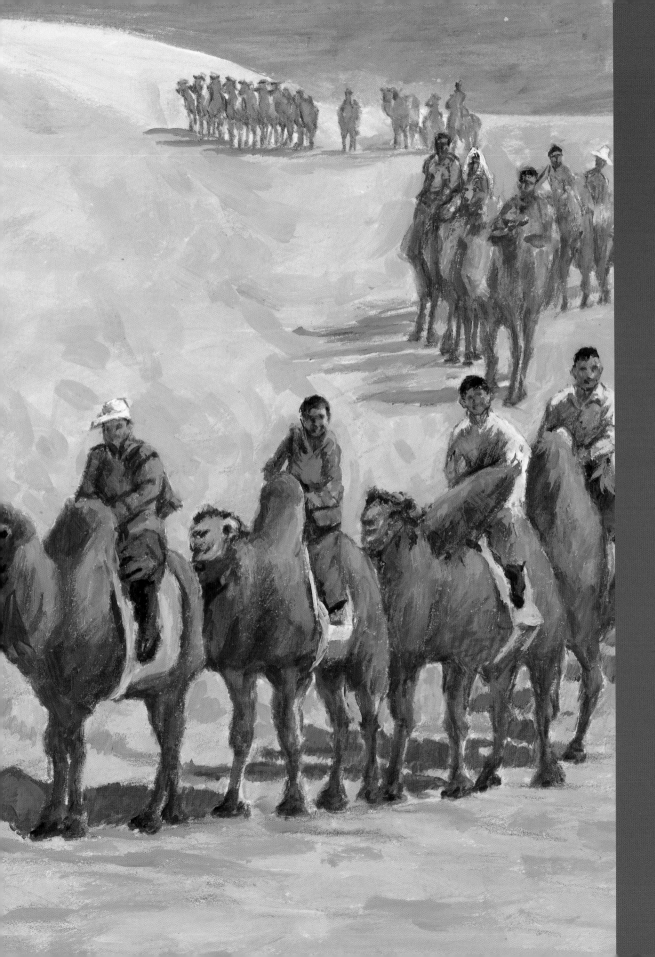

The story of how silk was discovered in China is a fascinating legend. An empress was watching the glistening cocoons that little worms were spinning in mulberry trees in the palace gardens. She unwound one of the threads of a cocoon and found that it was one very long strand of shiny material. She quickly pulled strands from several cocoons and found if put together they made a thicker thread. With the help of her ladies of the court, she spun the threads into one beautiful piece of cloth to make a robe for the emperor. Silk then became known as the royal cloth of kings.

The Chinese kept the secret of the silk-worms for over 2,500 years. The penalty for exporting, or selling, silk worms, or even telling where silk came from was death. Eventually the story of the silkworms was revealed to the West but China has always been the country with the most available silk. The production of silk thread gave the Chinese the art of embroidery. Today silk embroidery is practiced in nearly all regions of China. Silk fans, as well as scarves, jackets, and tablecloths, are decorated with many beautiful embroidered designs.

When the light turns red a whoosh of bicycles takes off. Pedaling a bicycle to travel around China is a must for vendors who use delivery bikes with carts, and for workers getting to their jobs. There are millions of bikes in China used for transporting goods. Think of a washer and dryer being delivered on the back of a bike! Many bikes with attached carts are used as market stalls. Vegetables, fruit, clothing, flowers, and "food-to-go" are a few of the items sold daily by the vendors. Tooting car horns are heard above the noises of the street. Drivers are always watching for bicycles in their path. Many people also use the public transportation systems such as buses, boats or ferries, trolleys, and trains.

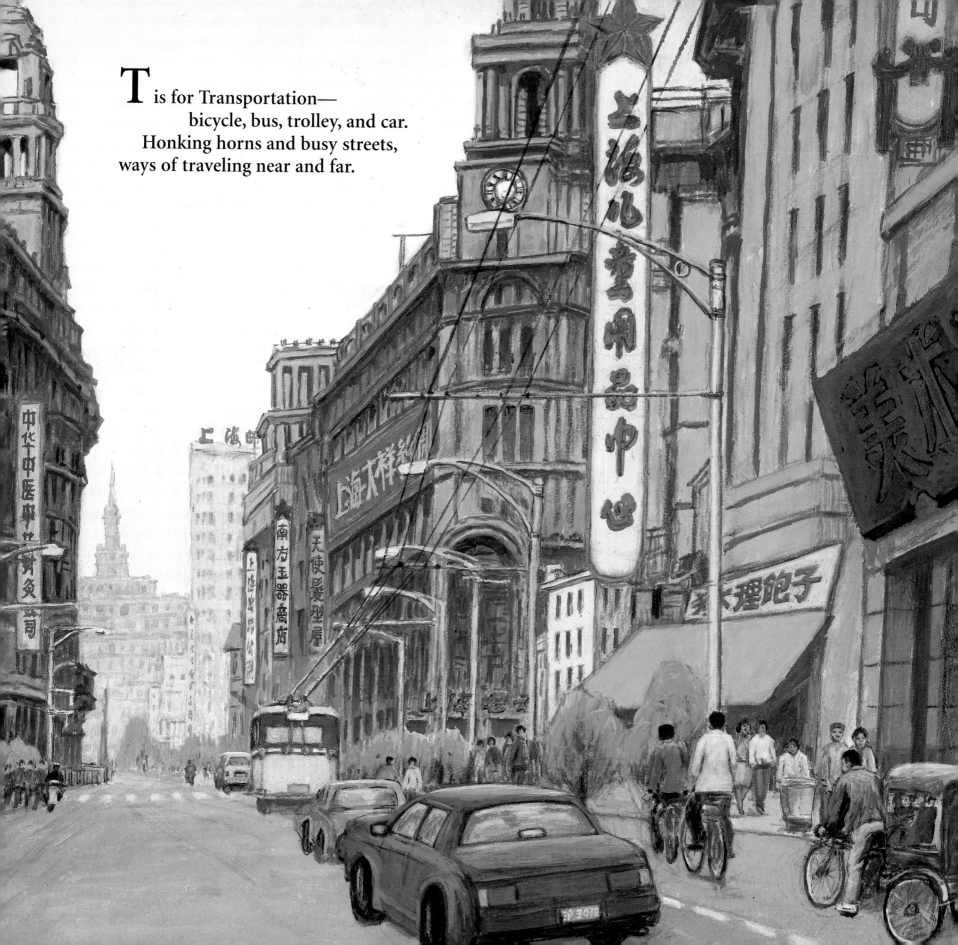

T is for Transportation—
bicycle, bus, trolley, and car.
Honking horns and busy streets,
ways of traveling near and far.

Have you ever gone to the circus and seen a wirewalker balance with an umbrella? Umbrellas are used worldwide for staying dry in rainy weather, or as parasols to give shade from the sun. Umbrellas are made from a variety of materials: silk, paper, nylon, or oilpaper. In China most have designs that are hand painted with birds, landscapes, flowers, and dragons. Some umbrellas are built on straight frames and some are collapsible. China is believed to be the home of the umbrella.

U is for Umbrella,
used in rain or shine.
Painted circles of paper or silk,
each with its own design.

U u

V is for Vegetables.
Bean sprouts and bamboo shoots,
eggplant, pea pods, and radishes
flavored with ginger roots.

V v

Children learn to love different types of vegetables at a very early age. Vegetables cooked with wonderful flavorings and rice are often the main course at every meal. Many people go daily to the outside market and pick out available vegetables. In China different seasons bring different vegetables. Some of the most popular are bok choy (a type of cabbage), snow peas, eggplant, bamboo, bean sprouts, onions, and spinach. These are prepared with mushrooms, ginger, and lotus roots and both white and black sesame seeds. Chop, chop, chop. You can hear families preparing vegetables for the evening meal. Do you like to eat vegetables?

Wok means cooking vessel. This cone-shaped cooking pan was designed years ago as a necessity in saving fuel and cooking fast. With its sloping sides and small cooking area, the pan concentrates the heat in a small space. Oil, which was a valuable cooking product, had to be used sparingly. The small cooking bottom used less oil and could be heated quickly. Many centuries ago fuel and food were scarce. To this day wok cooking is the most widely used form of cooking in China. In rural China heavy cast-iron woks are used in the ancient way. They are put in a pit over an open fire.

W
W

Used in stir-fry recipes
in meals around the clock,
W a bowl-shaped cooking pan—
is for wok.

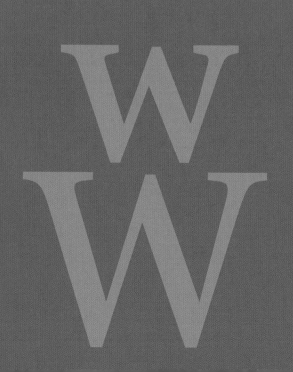

In China it is considered very important for all children to learn proper manners from a young age. In Mandarin Chinese, *Xiè xiè* (thank you) is pronounced "she-eh she-eh." *Ni hǎo* (hello) is pronounced "nee how." *Qing*, pronounced "cheeng," is how you say please. In Chinese sometimes the same word has several different meanings. It is the tone a word is spoken in that makes a difference in its meaning. The word *ma*, for example, can mean "mother," but said with a different tone it can mean "horse."

The spoken Chinese language has many different regional variations. However all variations of Chinese share the same grammar, vocabulary, and writing system. It is the pronunciation that is different. So two people from different regions may not be able to understand one another in speaking, but they would still be able to communicate by writing the symbols.

All schools in the People's Republic of China teach Standard Chinese, or Mandarin. Written Chinese is a language of symbols, but most modern dictionaries use the pīnyīn system. A daily newspaper may use 3,000 to 4,000 symbols.

X

X

X is for *xiè xiè*,
which means "thank you."
Ni hǎo means "hello," and
Ni hǎo ma is "how are you?"

The longest river in China is the Yangtze River. It is the third longest river in the world after the Amazon and the Nile. The river starts in the snow-covered mountains of Tibet, wanders eastward over the mainland of China, flows by the city of Shanghai, and empties into the East China Sea. The Yangtze River has been an important trade and transportation route since ancient times. Barges, sampans, junks, and cruise ships use the river and its tributaries for travel and pleasure. More than three million people live along the Yangtze River. Many crops, like rice, cotton, tea, silk, barley, and beans, are grown along the banks of the river.

Weaving a path through the mountains the river makes its way through the Three Gorges. These beautiful works of nature give breathtaking views of dangerous cliffs, waterfalls, and mountain peaks that reach the sky and surround the river with lush emerald green. Many varieties of fish that are rare and protected by the government are found in the river. The paddlefish, the Chinese sturgeon, and the peach fish come in schools when the peach trees are in bloom and are wonders of the Yangtze. Also found high in the mountains and natural areas along the river are many rare and unique animals, such as golden monkeys, white and black bears, Mandarin ducks, flying squirrels, the donkey-faced wolf, and giant salamanders.

The far-reaching Yangtze River
runs from the mountains to Shanghai.
The second longest is the Yellow River,
so these great rivers are our Y.

The Yellow River is the second largest river flowing through China. It was named so because the muddiness of the river makes the water look yellow. The Yellow River is the most silt-laden river in the world. It has been called "Mother River" as Chinese people have lived by and depended on the river for centuries. The Yellow River has also been called "China's Sorrow." Many floods have caused human suffering throughout the river's history. Flowing out of the mountains, it winds through landforms that provide very rich farmlands. The river is so diverse it is no wonder that it is called the Mother River.

The Chinese lunar calendar is based on the cycles of the moon. In the Chinese calendar the beginning of the year will fall somewhere between January and early February. The calendar is called a cyclical concept of time. To tell which month the calendar is in, every year is given an animal name or sign according to a repeating cycle. Rat, ox, tiger, rabbit, dragon, snake, horse, sheep, monkey, rooster, dog, and boar are the animal signs. Every 12 years the same animal name or sign will reappear.

Z z

Z is for the Chinese Zodiac.
Twelve animals are the signs.
The lunar cycles of the moon,
a calendar of circle designs.

Now let's have some zodiac fun.
Use the year you were born
to find your animal sign and see
how very special you can be.

1984 Rat
Imaginative, charming, and truly generous.

1985 Ox
Born leader and confident.

1986 Tiger
Sensitive and capable of great love.

1987 Rabbit
Affectionate, obliging, and always pleasant.

1988 Dragon
Intelligent, gifted, and a perfectionist.

1989 Snake
Rich in wisdom and charm.

1990 Horse
Hard worker, independent, and intelligent.

1991 Sheep
Charming, elegant, and artistic.

1992 Monkey
A clever wit, intelligent, and well liked.

1993 Rooster
Hard worker, shrewd, and decision maker.

1994 Dog
Honest, faithful, and a teacher.

1995 Boar
Good companion, sincere, and honest.

Can you find the sign for the year you were
born? (Hint) Remember the calendar has a
twelve-year cycle.

Carol Crane

Carol Crane is the author of twelve books with Sleeping Bear Press. In addition to *Dancing Dragon: A China Alphabet*, she has also written alphabet books for Florida, Texas, Alaska, Georgia, South Carolina, North Carolina, Alabama, and Delaware; and number books for South Carolina, North Carolina, Florida, and Texas. She is also the author of *P is for Pilgrim: A Thanksgiving Alphabet*. Carol is a historian and has always been a journal writer. She loves to stop and read historical markers. Traveling around the country, she speaks at reading conventions and schools, networking with children and educators on the fabric that makes up the quilt of this great country. Her greatest joy is to have a child say, "Wow! I didn't know that."

Zong-Zhou Wang

Zong-Zhou Wang was born in Shanxi Province in the People's Republic of China. He graduated from the Central University of Nationalities in Beijing, China with a major in fine art, specializing in oil painting. After graduation from the university, he was offered a position as one of the teaching faculty members. In 1988 he won First Prize in the First Nationwide Oil Painting Competition in China and The National Teacher's Painting Competition in Beijing, China. He is a member of the Chinese Artists Association, a prestigious academic organization of Chinese artists, and his paintings have been collected by the association for its permanent collection. This is one of the highest honors attainable by a Chinese artist. He is included in the Dictionary of the Achievements of World Chinese Artists, the Artists of Chinese Origin in North America Directory, and the World Famous Chinese Artist Almanac. His work has been exhibited all over the world. He currently lives in Philadelphia with his family.